# JONAH AND THE WHALE

**Read-Along Storybook**
**Sing-Along Songs • PC Fun!**

Published by

PC Multimedia Entertainment
TREASURES, INC.

2765 Metamora Road, Oxford, Michigan 48371 USA

### Jonah and the Whale
Story adapted by Darcy Weinbeck
Audio CD Reading Performed by David DuChene
Songs Produced and Performed by Deron (D.B.) Harris
Vocal Performances by Melissa Cusick and Deron (D.B.) Harris

ISBN 978-1600720932

First Published 2008

Long ago, there lived a man of God named Jonah. One day God told Jonah to go to the city of Nineveh and tell the wicked people there to stop their evil ways.

TURN PAGE

Jonah was fearful of going to Nineveh because the people that lived there were not very nice. Jonah was not looking forward to the dangerous mission God had chosen for him.

After thinking about God's request, Jonah decided to pack for the journey to Nineveh. He doubted he could do much to change the people there, and thought that if the trip became too perilous, he could always turn around and return home.

It was with much doubt and fear that Jonah started on his journey. Part way there, Jonah came upon a fork in the road. One road led to Nineveh and the other road led to the seacoast town of Joppa.

Jonah gave in to his fears and decided to take the road to Joppa. From there he hoped to find a boat that would take him far away from God and the dangerous city of Nineveh.

TURN PAGE

"One ticket please…to anywhere," Jonah said as he arrived at the pier in Joppa. Jonah paid the fare for the next ship scheduled to leave. The ship was sailing for the city of Tarshish. Jonah quickly boarded the ship.

Jonah thought he was very clever. "What better place to hide from the Lord than out at sea?" he thought. But Jonah forgot the very important fact that God was always there by his side, every moment of every day. There was nothing Jonah could do to escape God or His great plan for him.

TURN PAGE

God decided to remind Jonah that He is always present. He sent a windstorm over the sea that rocked the boat wildly. The other passengers on the boat bent down on their knees and cried out to their gods in fear. They wanted to know why they were being punished.

Concerned for themselves and the other passengers, the crew members went from person to person, asking each of them if they had, in some way, angered God.

When the crewmen approached Jonah and asked if he had angered God, Jonah hung his head sadly and answered, "Yes, I have disobeyed God and now I am running away from Him. But it is obvious to me that there is no escaping the will of the Lord. I have risked your lives as well as my own."

Jonah sighed and told the crew members, "Throw me overboard and God will calm the sea. He is upset with me, not you. Save yourselves and send me to my fate."

The crew members felt sorry for Jonah. Rather than throw him overboard, they decided to row through crashing waves that grew higher and stronger with each passing moment.

As the waves grew even more powerful and the boat was on the verge of sinking, the crewmen decided that they had no choice but to throw Jonah overboard. Jonah splashed into the sea and watched as the waters around the boat calmed as it sailed away.

Jonah was relieved that the boat and its passengers were safe, though he was very worried to be all alone so far out at sea. Jonah decided that his only choice was to try to swim back to the town of Joppa.

While Jonah was swimming towards the distant shore, he was unaware that he was not alone in the water. Coming up from behind him was a huge whale. It swam closer and closer until it was just a few feet away.

TURN PAGE

Jonah was startled when the whale made a terrific splash just behind him. Jonah cried out, "Dear God, I have failed you in your mission. I have been weak and have lacked courage. Now do with me what you will. I deserve nothing more than to be swallowed up by this whale."

Accepting his fate, Jonah turned to face the whale. He could see his own reflection in its huge eye and he barely recognized his own appearance. He looked small, weak, and scared.

TURN PAGE

Jonah said to the whale, "If you are hungry, please put me out of my misery. I deserve nothing more than to be eaten by you." God spoke to the whale and told it to swallow Jonah whole.

The whale's stomach was so large that Jonah could stand up straight and still not reach the top. There was no escape, so Jonah did the only thing he could do. He knelt down and began to pray.

TURN PAGE

"Dear God," Jonah said, "I have sinned against you. I did not go to Nineveh as you told me to. I did not warn them of the dangers of their evil ways. And so, I am just as guilty for their sins as they are. Dear God, please forgive me."

After three days and three nights inside the whale, Jonah heard a loud rumbling from within and he was sure that it meant his end was near. He sat with his eyes closed, desiring with all of his heart that he had been a better person in life and that he had spent more time being close with God.

After another loud rumble Jonah found himself caught in a terrific wave that carried him out of the whale's stomach. The wave was of such force that it hurled Jonah almost to the shore. Jonah stumbled onto the sandy beach.

With renewed spirit and faith, Jonah began to walk toward the city of Nineveh. He was looking forward to doing God's work and showing God how grateful he was for all of His wonderful gifts.

TURN PAGE

NINEVEH →

When Jonah arrived in Nineveh, he spoke with such strong belief that all of the townspeople listened intently. As he spoke of God's loving and merciful ways he noticed his reflection in a nearby pond. He saw not the weak, frail man reflected in the whale's eye, but rather the reflection of a man filled with the strength that only God can provide.

# SAMSON AND DELILAH

Read-Along Storybook
Sing-Along Songs
PC Fun!

# Noah's Ark

Read-Along Storybook · Sing-Along Songs · PC Fun!

# Enjoy All 4 Stories!

Read-Along Storybook
Sing-Along Songs · PC Fun!

# JONAH AND THE WHALE

SING-ALONG SONGS · PC FUN!

# DAVID AND GOLIATH